Let's ditch the prejudiced labeling, and embrace our Human Race for its diversity, inclusivity, equity and individuality we all deserve.

It's Me

Jeff Kubiak

Illustrated by Briannah Altpeter

It's Me
By Jeff Kubiak
Illustrated by Briannah Altpeter
Published by EduMatch®
PO Box 150324, Alexandria, VA 22315

www.edumatch.org

ISBN-13: 978-1-970133-99-8

Foreword

Every human on the planet—at sometime or another—questions their worth or sense of belonging. This is especially true for children and adolescents. Growing up, I thought there was something inherently wrong with me because I struggled to keep myself organized, remember where I put things, manage my time, and focus on what was important rather than just what was interesting. When I knew that there was a name for what I was experiencing and that I wasn't alone, I felt a tremendous amount of relief and empowered to focus on leveraging my strengths over constantly focusing on how I was different from my peers. I wish I'd had Jeff's book back then. I bet all my classmates would have benefited from it too. *It's Me* is a reminder that the one thing that we all have in common—that truly brings us together—is that we are all individuals ... worthy and remarkable in our own ways *because* of our uniqueness, not in spite of it.

Amy Fast Ed.D.
Educator, Author, and Education Commentator

Thank you for choosing to read *It's Me.* The vignettes in this book are real stories, written by students, teachers, and educators. Some of the names have been changed or kept anonymous.

It's not easy to "see people" for who they are, let alone embrace them. But now, more than ever, we need to allow ourselves and others the opportunity to not only see, but to "be seen," and truly welcome differing views, cultures, and characteristics.

Currently, our Mental Health Services are depleted, teen suicide rates are skyrocketing, depression and drug use are increasing, and schools seem to be coming up short with support systems and resources, due to financial strains. Many times, students with the most critical needs are being overlooked and underserved.

The time to change is now. When empathy, understanding, and compassion become an intentional part of our purpose, we are more able to accept, embrace, and celebrate the uniqueness of all.

Taking the time to learn each other's stories and to be more informed will allow our compassion and enlightenment to grow. When this happens, we find common ground.

Communication does not equal agreement, but it CAN equal compassion, understanding, and acceptance.

Jeff Kubiak

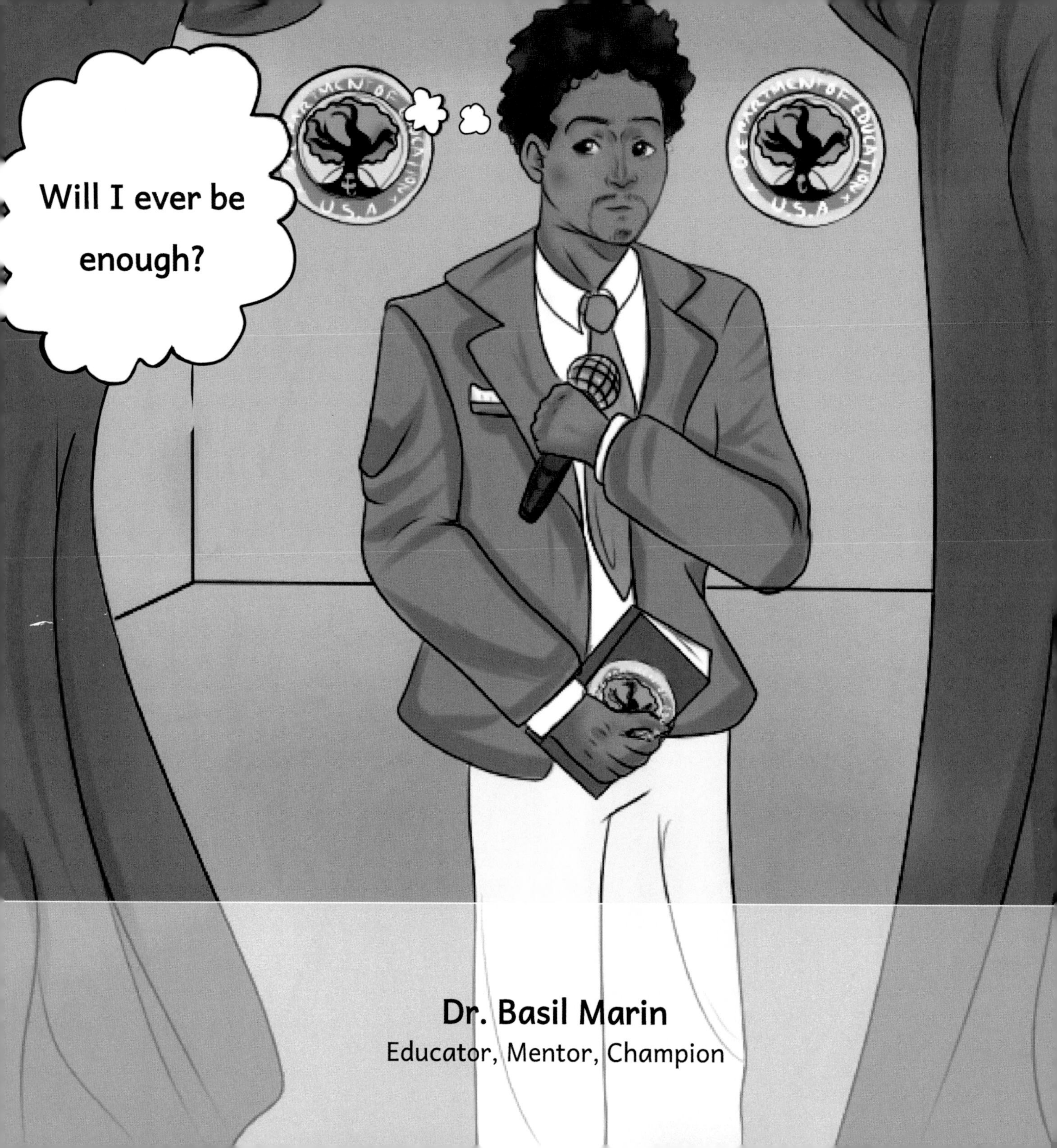
Will I ever be enough?

Dr. Basil Marin
Educator, Mentor, Champion

It's Me

Yes, I am a Black male.
Does my skin scare you;
do you see me as a threat?

If you get to know me, you will learn that
I am a big teddy bear and,
I love music and sports.

I often times ponder, "Will I ever be enough?
Why do I have to work twice as hard
to be seen and recognized?"

I do not want to be seen or
Viewed as a statistic; however,
I am a part of the 2% of educators
who are Black men.
I am a part of the 2%
of all individuals who hold a doctoral degree.

I am human and I want to use my
Black Skin to make a positive
difference in the world.

My skin is not a threat, it is a strength.
It's me.

Braden, age 12,
an amazing boy with ADHD

It's Me

I know, I can't sit still,
I want to do so much.

I can be overwhelming to lots of people,
Because I move all the time.

So many thoughts are racing
through my mind,
But my brain just won't slow down.

I try so hard - but I have lots of energy.
Please don't yell at me,
I'm trying my best.

Watch me thrive, I am a master at selling!
Lemonade, rocks, or inventions,
I can sell it all!

It's me.

Carmen, age 16,
suffers from depression

It's Me

I hate how I look.
People think I'm ugly,
So I sit in the corner quietly.

They call me "Fatso" and "Tubby,"
Even my mom says I'm fat.

Depression really weighs me down,
I feel so sad and alone.

But I'm kind, thoughtful and caring,
and I'm a great musician.

I can make the best vegan lasagna,
Want to come over sometime?

Yes, it's me.

Britney, age 11,
has dyslexia and a processing disorder

It's Me

Sometimes, I strggel,
and dont alwys "get it."

It dusnt mean I'm not smrt,
but, kids laff at my mistakes.

I just cnt process stuf as fast as you,
reeding and speleen is hard for me.

Letters, nmbers and thoughts are mixd,
and I get confusd.

I'm vry creativ and knd,
give me a chans, please.

It's me.

Alex, age 14,
has PTSD from being verbally abused

It's Me

I'm the one who loses my temper,
then breaks your crayons.

I sometimes tear up papers,
and yell real loud.

My anger comes so quickly,
I just can't hold it in.

Just like when my dad is mean to me,
I want you to feel my pain.

Please give me time to calm down,
I really don't try to be this way.

I have a great sense of humor,
and I love animals.

It's me.

Esther, age 15,
has low self-esteem and suffers from Bulimia

It's Me

I'm the worst at everything,
I just can't help it.

I don't mean to mess up,
but I'm just no good.

Do I look pretty to you?
Am I ugly?

Did you know I love to design clothing?
I want to look like a celebrity.

Sometimes I eat too much,
Then I make myself sick.

Can you please help?
I'm not sure what to do.

It's me.

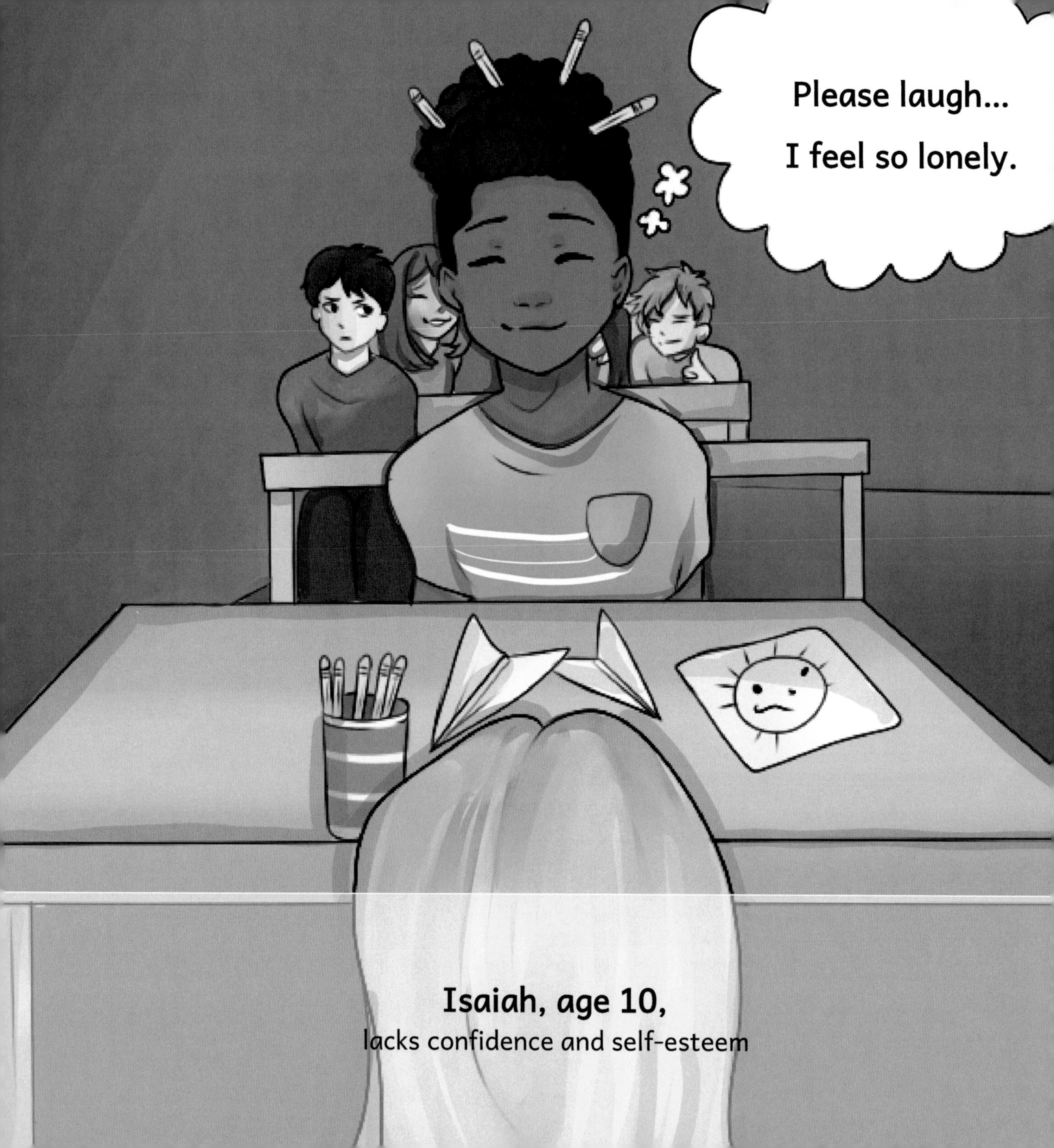
Please laugh...
I feel so lonely.

Isaiah, age 10,
lacks confidence and self-esteem

It's Me

I love to joke and make fun of people,
but I don't have much confidence.

I want people to like me,
and getting laughs makes me feel important.

I don't mean to hurt you,
when I make jokes and tease.

I don't get much attention at home,
so a giggle makes me feel good...I think.

Did you know I'm an amazing writer?
Would you like to read my stuff?

It's me.

Oscar, age 13,
a misunderstood, shy introvert

It's Me

No one ever notices me,
because I'm so quiet.

But people make fun,
because I love to sit and read.
Quiet time helps me recharge.

I get uncomfortable around people,
and large groups are so overwhelming.

I love to climb trees and take photos.
Some of my pictures have even been in a
magazine!

It's me!

Ameerah, age 13,
a proud Muslim American, but often prejudged and not given a chance

Hi, it's Me

I wear a hijab on my head,
I know it looks different.

I am a Muslim American,
but it doesn't mean I am submissive,
or promote violence.

I am like other girls,
and love to laugh and play.

Science excites me so much,
I want to be a chemist
like Dr. Marie Maynard Daly!

Please see past my looks.
And really see Me.

It's me.

Elijah, age 16,
a hard-working African American male, often judged only by his skin color

It's Me!

I know I seem confident and sure,
but, do you know how hard I work?
Or, how my dad pushes me?

I study before school, and late at night,
I'm not perfect.
And so tired of the pressure.

I have friends, skills, and love to win,
but it's not as easy as it seems.
I'm so afraid to fail.

Get to know me.
I am kind, genuine, and smart too.

It's me.

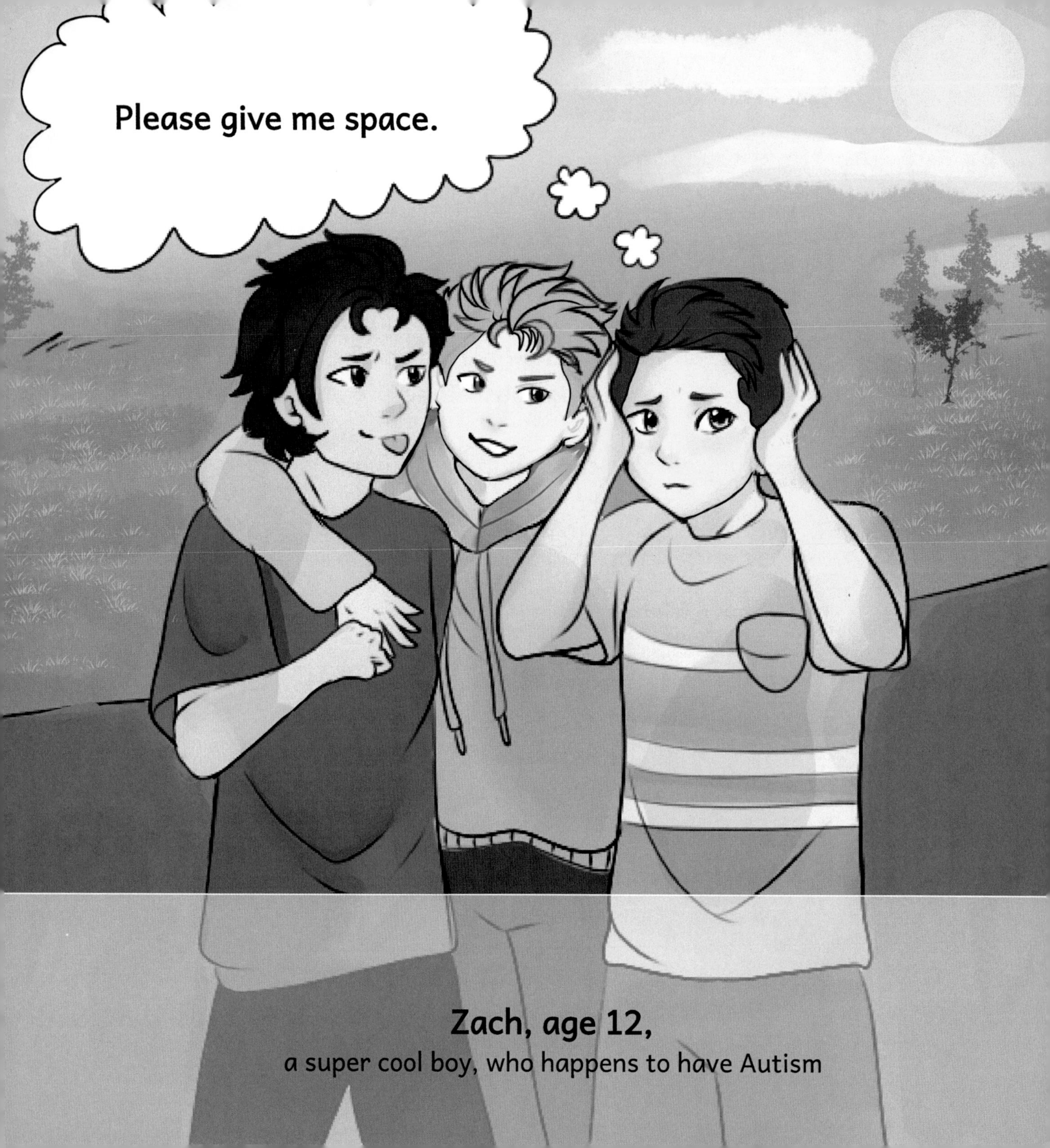
Please give me space.

Zach, age 12,
a super cool boy, who happens to have Autism

It's Me

Please don't get so close to me,
I don't like to look at people.

I might repeat the same thing, over and over.
People say I'm on "The Spectrum"
and "weird."

Routines really help me,
but I don't like when it's too loud.

I'm honest and passionate,
about things that interest me.

Ask me anything about airplanes,
I can tell you so much!

It's me.

María, trece años,
orgullosamente Latina

Maria, age 13,
a proud Latina

Soy Yo

Sí, yo hablo otra lengua.
Eso no significa que no soy inteligente.
O que no puedo solucionar problemas.

Por favor sé paciente mientras yo
aprendo
Hablar recio no ayuda.
No soy sorda.
Estoy traduciendo en mi mente y
eso toma tiempo.

¿Sabías que yo era la mejor
estudiante de mi clase en mi país

Soy yo.

It's Me

Yes, I speak another language.
It doesn't mean I'm not smart.
Or I can't figure things out.

Please, be patient as I learn.
Speaking loudly doesn't help.
I'm not deaf.
I am just translating in my head,
and
it takes time.

Did you know I was at the
top of my class in my country?

It's me.

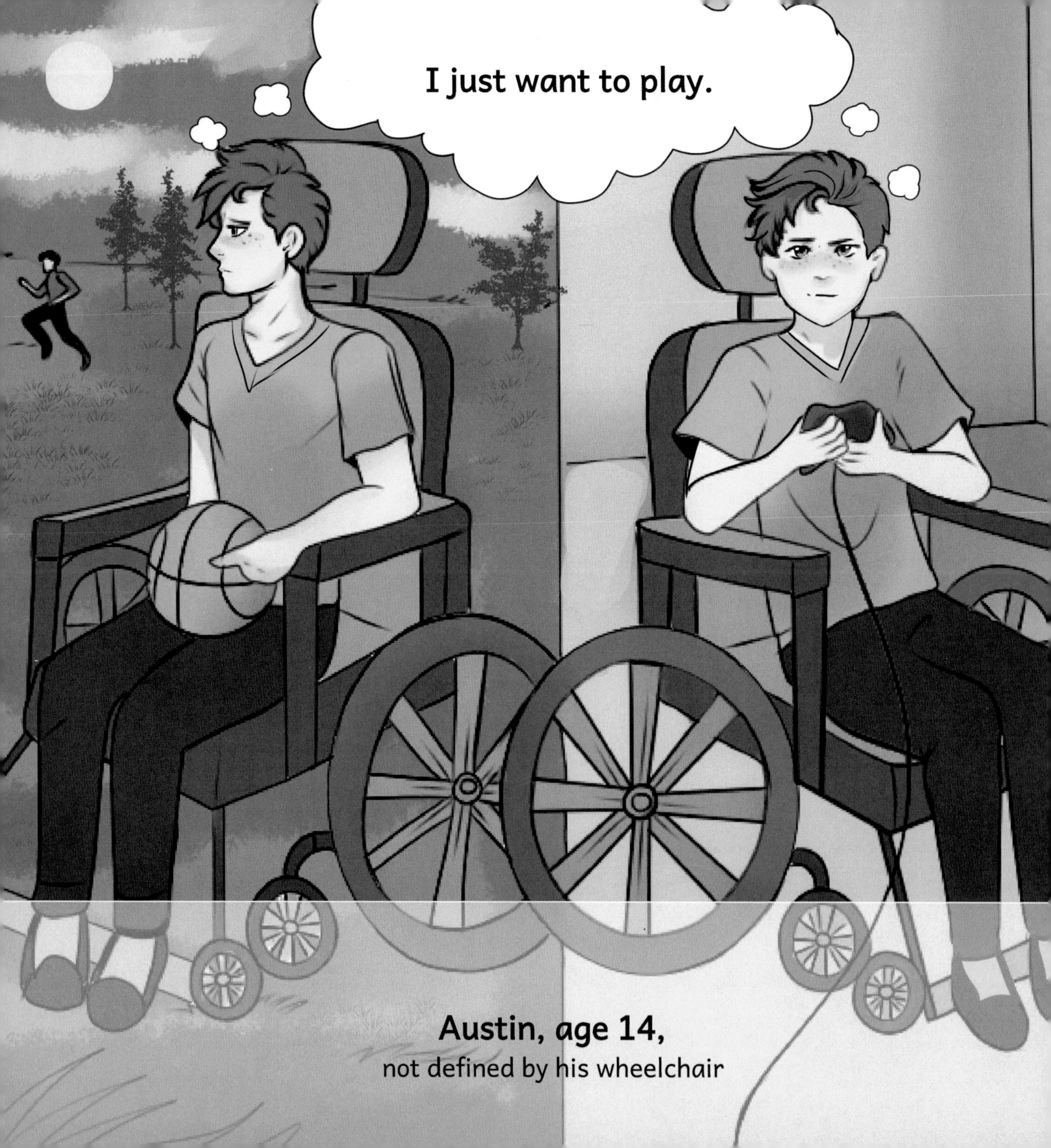
I just want to play.

Austin, age 14,
not defined by his wheelchair

It's Me

I'm in a wheelchair.
But, I promise, you can't "catch"
what I have.

I love playing games.
I just can't use my legs,
the way you do.

Can we be friends?
I can do so many things,
if you give me a chance!

Did you know that I am a paralympic
basketball player?

Look — it's me!

Amber, age 17,
pressured to always be perfect

It's Me

The teachers all love ME the most.
So, do NOT copy my work or I'll tell!

My parents put me down if I'm not perfect.
So I make others feel bad too.

Daddy says I MUST go to Harvard.
He thinks that is all that matters.

How come no one ever invites me over?
I love to cook, but I burn everything.

Is it ok to fail?
I'd really love to have a friend.

It's me.

Jung, age 11,
wants to learn in more than one way

It's Me

Can't I just build and create things?
I learn by doing and tinkering with machines.

Please, no worksheets or memorizing lame
facts,
or tutors and extra teachers.

Hear my words please,
I will make you proud!

Let me use my hands to design,
code, and invent!

I've created my own video games,
and a robot—you wanna play?

It's me.

Shondra, age 12,
a foster child who wants to feel loved

It's Me

Yes, I know my clothes aren't clean,
but, did you know I've had
six homes in three years?

Mom left because of drug problems,
and bad things happen to me.

I don't have much,
but my heart is big.
Will you help me?

I want to be an artist or designer.
I have so much love I want to give.

It's me.

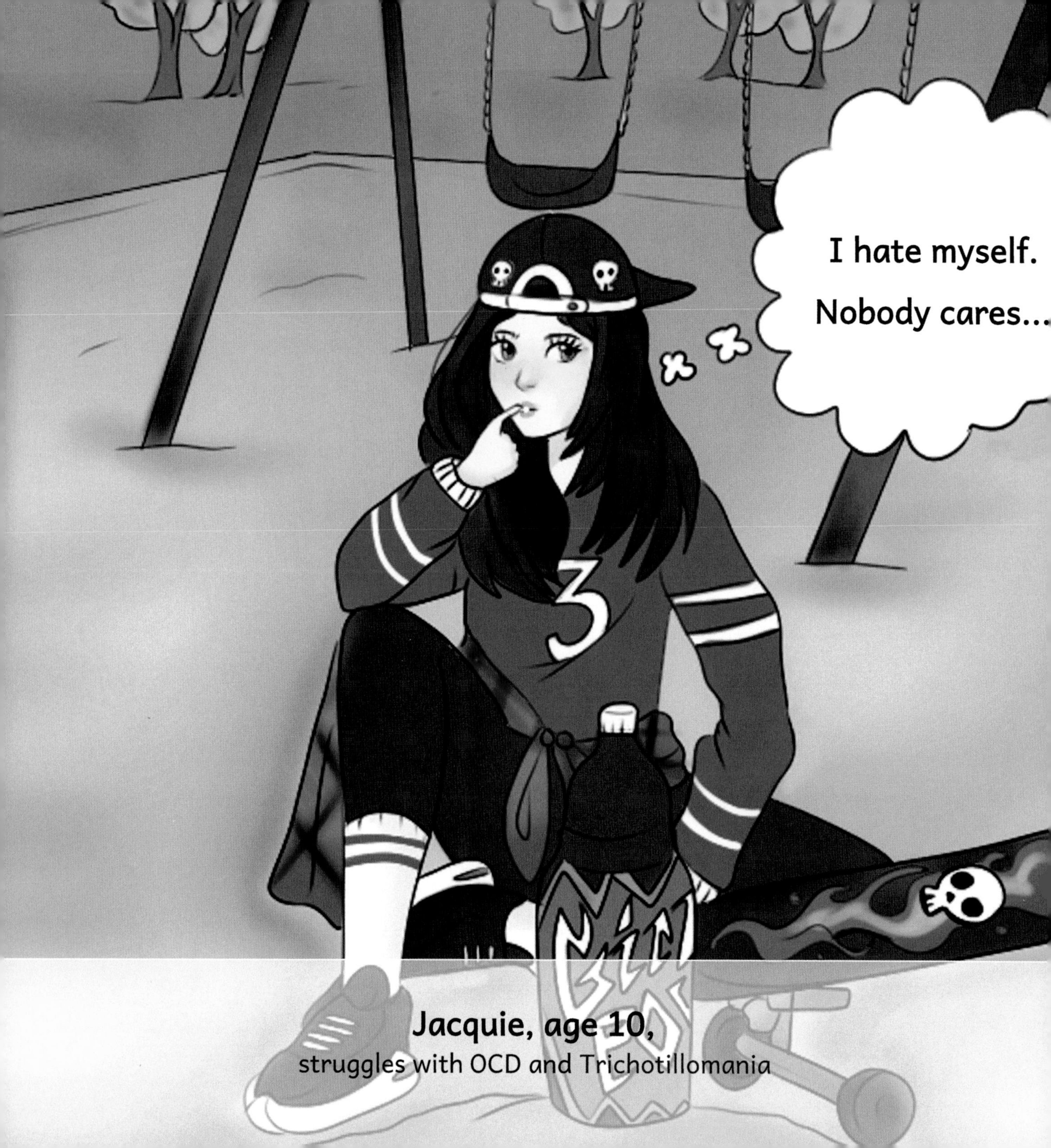
I hate myself.
Nobody cares...

Jacquie, age 10,
struggles with OCD and Trichotillomania

It's Me

I might seem fine to you,
But, did you know I can't sleep?

I bite my nails, and pull my hair out.
Sometimes, I hate myself.

No one "gets me"— but they all say
"we understand."

I keep having negative, repetitive thoughts.
Can you help me?
What is wrong?

I love making funny videos,
and I want to skate in the Olympics!

Yes, it's me.

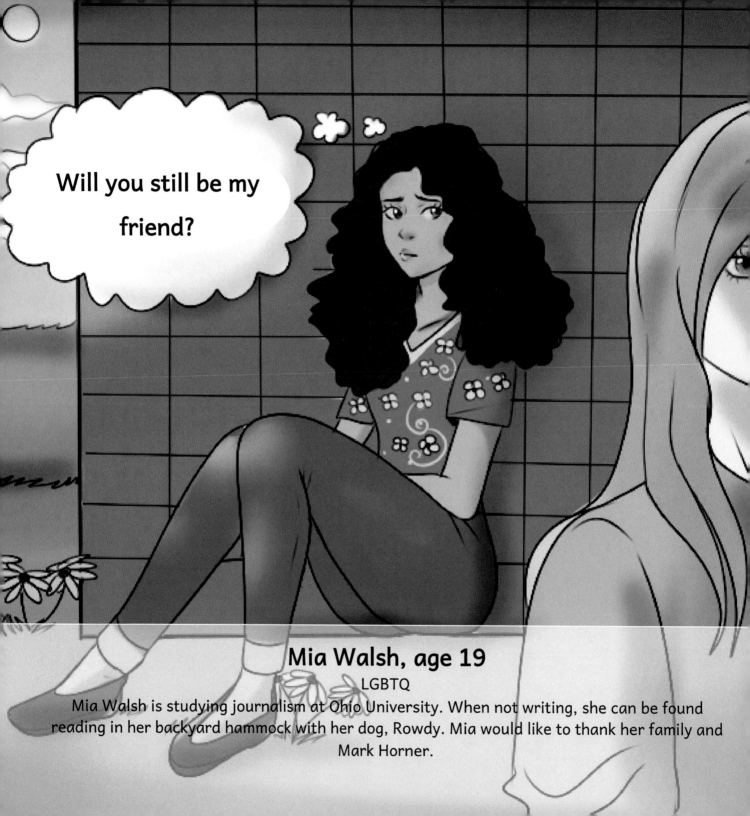

Mia Walsh, age 19

LGBTQ

Mia Walsh is studying journalism at Ohio University. When not writing, she can be found reading in her backyard hammock with her dog, Rowdy. Mia would like to thank her family and Mark Horner.

Hello - It's Me!

I am in your class, and I love to smile.
I want to run, I want to play!

I'm just like you, but I'm a girl
who doesn't like boys.

It's not like I chose this.
I'm still just a kid.

People say I'm weird and call me names,
all because of who I like.

I love playing guitar and writing
for the school paper!
Will you be my friend?

After all, it's just me.

MacKenna, age 16,
a regular teen, with Tourette's Syndrome

It's Me

I'm the kid that twitches and has tics,
please don't be so quick to judge.

Some people think I'm weird,
but, I'm a normal teen, just like you.
I still love to be silly and have fun.

This only affects my movements,
not my happiness.

So trust me when I say,
you can't "catch it."

Can I do your makeup, or style
your clothes?

It's me.

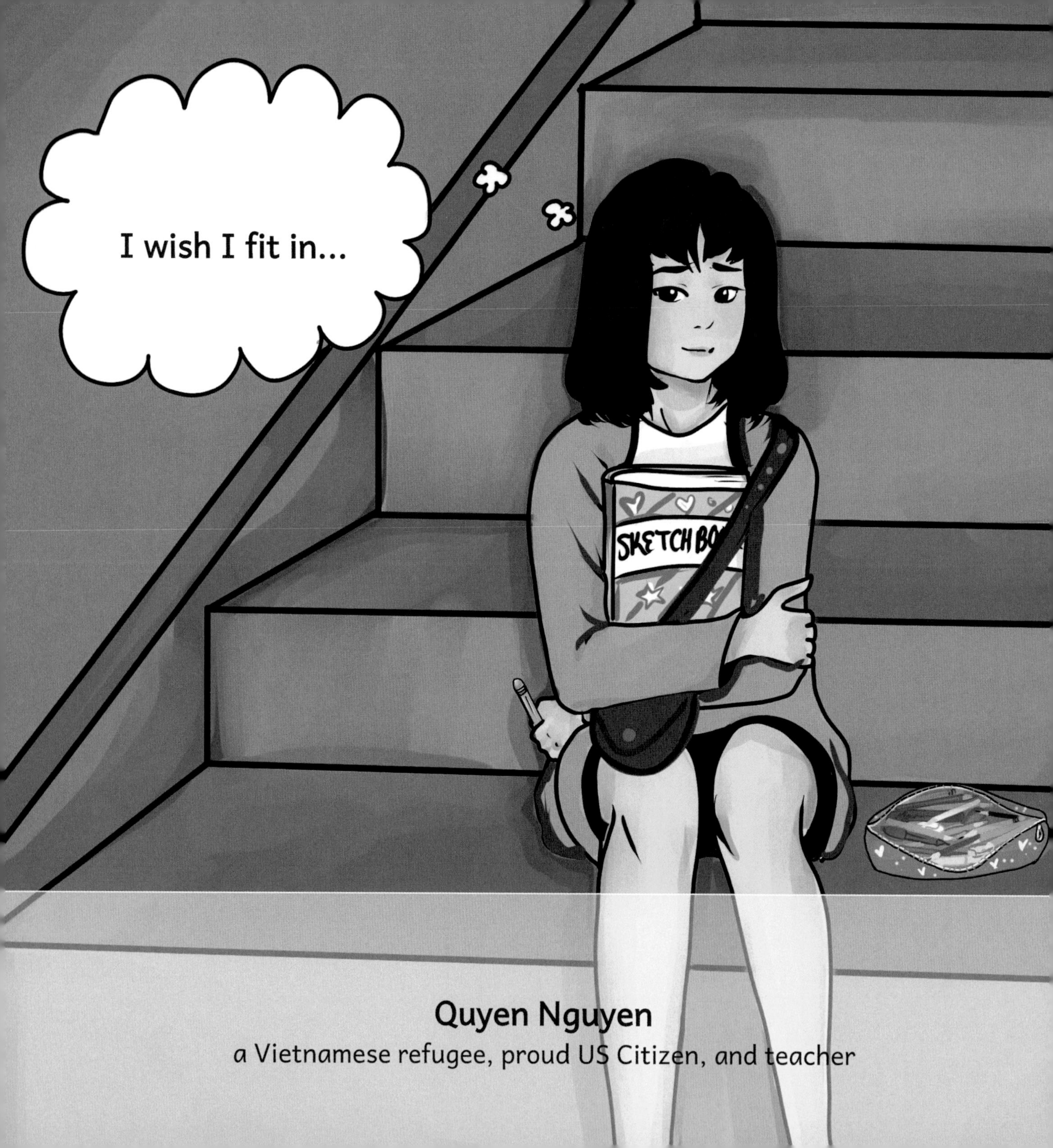
I wish I fit in...
SKETCHBO

Quyen Nguyen

a Vietnamese refugee, proud US Citizen, and teacher

It's Me

Do you wonder why I look and speak
differently than everyone else?

I am teased and taunted.
I had to leave my war-torn country,

Will you accept me?
I just want to fit in!

I hope I am given a chance to succeed
like many others.

Did you know I love to create art
and teach kids to read?

It's me.

Melanie Korach
Teacher, Mother, and #StarfishClub Founder

It's Me

I'm your teacher.
I see you.

I want you to know I care about you,
and support you with kindness and empathy.

I will challenge you to be your best.
I want to know your story better,
And get to know YOU.

I believe in you and want you to succeed.
I'm not perfect either,
and I make mistakes too.

I Love You
I support You

It's me.

Gratitude

I could not have done this work without many amazing people in my life. Thank you to: Basil Marin, Mia Walsh, Keeley Kubiak, Braden Kubiak, Piper Kubiak, Sarah Thomas, Bri Altpeter, Nicole Biscotti, my book focus group, and all of the amazing people that participated in this passion project. There are so many educators and students I have known and learned from over the years, that have brought joy and passion to my life.

Keep including, accepting, embracing, and being an equitable voice. You are the difference!

***

"Effective Diversity efforts must represent mirrors and windows; a space where ALL people see themselves [mirrors] AND connect with others [windows] in ways that support fostering an equitable society."
Dr. Derrick Gay
Dr. Rudine Sims Bishops

"How far you go in life depends on your being tender with the young, compassionate with the aged, sympathetic with the striving and tolerant of the weak and strong. Because someday in your life you will have been all of these."
George Washington Carver

Glossary of Terms

ADHD – Attention Deficit Hyperactivity Disorder is a common condition that's caused by differences in the brain. People with ADHD have trouble with focus. But some are also hyperactive and impulsive. That's especially true with kids and teens.
It's not clear exactly how many people in the United States have ADHD, but estimates are between 5 and 11 percent. https://www.nimh.nih.gov/

Anxiety Disorder – an emotion characterized by feelings of tension, worried thoughts, and physical changes like increased blood pressure. People with anxiety disorders usually have recurring intrusive thoughts or concerns. They may avoid certain situations out of worry. They may also have physical symptoms such as sweating, trembling, dizziness, or a rapid heartbeat. https://www.apa.org/topics/anxiety

Autism - a neurodevelopmental disorder that affects how kids process certain types of information. Autism is lifelong. You don't grow out of it. People with autism tend to have common challenges, such as: social skills, communication and language, processing of information, repetitive behaviors or movements, and a need for routine, among other things. https://www.autismspeaks.org/what-autism

Bulimia – an emotional disorder involving distortion of body image and an obsessive desire to lose weight, in which bouts of extreme overeating are followed by depression and self-induced vomiting, purging, or fasting.
https://www.nationaleatingdisorders.org/learn/by-eating-disorder/bulimia

Depression - Depression (major depressive disorder) is a common and serious medical illness that negatively affects how you feel, the way you think, and how you act. Depression causes feelings of sadness and/or a loss of interest in activities once enjoyed. It can lead to a variety of emotional and physical problems and can decrease a person's ability to function at work and at home. https://www.psychiatry.org

Dyslexia - Dyslexia is a specific learning disability that is neurobiological in origin. It is characterized by difficulties with accurate and/or fluent word recognition and by poor spelling and decoding abilities. Consequences may include problems in reading comprehension and reduced reading experience that can impede growth of vocabulary and background knowledge. https://dyslexiaida.org/definition-of-dyslexia/

Hijab - is an Arabic word meaning barrier or partition. It is the traditional covering for the hair and neck that is worn by Muslim women. https://study.com/academy/lesson/hijab-definition-and-relation-to-islam.html

Introvert - a reserved or shy person who enjoys spending time alone. Also, may be uncomfortable in social groups. https://www.merriam-webster.com/dictionary/introvert

LGBTQ - is an acronym for lesbian, gay, bisexual, transgender and queer or questioning. These terms are used to describe a person's sexual orientation or gender identity. https://gaycenter.org/about/lgbtq/

OCD - **Obsessive-Compulsive Disorder,** is a common, chronic, and long-lasting disorder in which a person has uncontrollable, reoccurring thoughts (obsessions) and/or behaviors (compulsions) that he or she feels the urge to repeat over and over. https://www.nimh.nih.gov/health/topics/obsessive-compulsive-disorder-ocd

PTSD - Posttraumatic stress disorder (PTSD) is a psychiatric disorder that may occur in people who have experienced or witnessed a traumatic event such as a natural disaster, a serious accident, a terrorist act, war/combat, or violence of any kind. https://www.psychiatry.org/patients-families/ptsd/what-is-ptsd

Tourette's Syndrome - is a disorder that involves repetitive movements or unwanted sounds (tics) that can't be easily controlled. For instance, you might repeatedly blink your eyes, shrug your shoulders, or blurt out unusual sounds or words. https://tourette.org/about-tourette/overview/what-is-tourette/

Trichotillomania - also called hair-pulling disorder, is a mental disorder that involves recurrent, irresistible urges to pull out hair from your scalp, eyebrows or other areas of your body, despite trying to stop. https://www.mayoclinic.org/diseases-conditions/trichotillomania/symptoms-causes/syc-20355188

Resources

While this list is not inclusive of all resources, I hope you find these helpful. Please don't hesitate to reach out for help. Asking for help is one of life's biggest strengths.

- National Suicide Prevention Hotline - 1-800-273-8255, https://suicidepreventionlifeline.org/
- Mental Health Network - https://www.mhn.com/, 1-800-662-HELP (4357)
- Overeaters Anonymous - https://oa.org/
- National Eating Disorders - https://www.nationaleatingdisorders.org/help-support/covid-19-resources-page
- CHADD - Children and Adults with ADD/ADHD - https://chadd.org/
- Tourette Association of America - https://tourette.org/about-tourette/overview/what-is-tourette/
- Southern Poverty Law Center (Anti Racism Network) - https://www.splcenter.org/
- National Alliance on Mental Illness (PTSD, Anxiety, Bipolar, Eating Disorders, Depression and others) https://www.nami.org/About-Mental-Illness/Mental-Health-Conditions/Posttraumatic-Stress-Disorder
- English Learner Resources - US. Department of Education - https://www2.ed.gov/about/offices/list/ocr/ell/edlite-otherresources.html https://www.ncela.ed.gov/external-resources

About the Author

Jeff is a father, son, brother, husband, and loyal friend. His first book, *One Drop of Kindness,* is an award winning children's book that helps share the message that everyone has kindness inside of them, but some need help to find it.

Jeff has been an elite swimmer, a coach, and an educator around the globe and most currently in Northern California. He loves spending time in the outdoors with his family. Jeff strives to make education equitable and inclusive for all.

You can contact him at: www.jeffkubiak.com, @jeffreykubiak (Twitter), @Jeffkubiakauthor (Instagram), and his books are available on Amazon, Barnes and Noble, and other outlets.

About the Illustrator

Briannah is a freelance illustrator born and raised in Ontario, Canada. Briannah always had a passion for art and began illustrating professionally at age sixteen when she created avatars for the *First In Math* online educational program by engineer Robert Sun of Suntex International. In her free time, Briannah enjoys writing, drawing for pleasure, and playing video games with her friends. Briannah describes herself as a storyteller and strives to tell a story through any medium. Aside from art, she is a strong believer in equality. Briannah believes our differences should be embraced and that no one should be ashamed of being themselves.

Dr. Basil Marin is currently an Assistant Principal at Chamblee Charter High School in Atlanta, Georgia. His previous roles include alternative special education classroom teacher and lead behavioral specialist. In his current role, Dr. Marin is charged with leading the school improvement process, Title I implementation, increasing family engagement, and communication with ELL parents and students. You will often find him presenting at conferences speaking to his passions, such as equity in education, social-emotional learning, and whole-child approaches to education. Dr. Marin recently graduated from the Educational Leadership program at Old Dominion University. Dr. Marin looks forward to connecting with like-minded individuals who are also passionate about disrupting the status quo.

Endorsements

Empathy is a revelatory antidote to hate. In *It's Me*, Kubiak MASTERFULLY reminds us that everyone has a valuable story worth uncovering when we take the time to lean in to curiosity and vulnerability. Perhaps, the most powerful takeaway in this BRILLIANT social emotional learning gem is that we as humans--are all universally seeking the same love, attention, and support to help us chase our dreams. I highly recommend this OUTSTANDING picture book to children of all ages as a solution to our world's disconnection, mental health crisis, and social unrest!

-Hans Appel, counselor, speaker, podcaster, and author of *Award Winning Culture*

Jeff does it again! A book that touches your heart and makes you think about the importance of loving and valuing everyone buying what we physically see. This book will make you reflect on the real challenges many experiencing daily. *It's Me* is so needed as we become agents of change; showing kindness and empathy to others.

-Lynmara Colón, Transformative Educator, Co-Author of *Empower our Girls*, and presenter

It's Me is the book that not only our students need to read in today's world, but ALL humans! Every single one of us has insecurities, fears, self-doubt, and characteristics out of our control that make us who we are. *It's Me* breaks through the walls, each page is filled with a description that pulls at your heartstrings and brings a tear to your eye from characters from all walks of life. We don't know what is truly going on inside other's minds and hearts, but Jeff does a phenomenal job of bringing awareness to what we may overlook at times. I am grateful to have a friend like Jeff Kubiak that is determined to change our world for the better. I will walk with him on this mission, which *It's Me* will begin. I hope you will join us.

-Michael Earnshaw, Father, Husband, Principal, Author, Skateboarder, & Marathoner that is determined to change to world.

When creators create, a part of them is always infused into what they make. One word that comes to mind when I think of Jeff Kubiak is, authentic. No doubt, his second book *It's Me* earnestly attempts to communicate authenticity through the people he has brought to life in his writing. Their vulnerability and quest to be seen stands out from cover to cover. I pray this book moves us closer to being a more transparent, honest and authentic people. Enjoy!
-Dennis Mathew, Author of *Bello the Cello*, *My Wild First Day of School*, Father, Anti Racist, and influencer.

It's Me is a beautiful series of voices that shares the importance of accepting each other while appreciating what each of us brings to better our school communities. This gives a perspective too often we don't always see. Jeff continues to share his heart while amplifying student voices in every word.
-Jessica Cabeen, Award Winning Principal, Author of *Hacking Early Learning*, *Lead with Grace, Unconventional Leadership*, and Co-Author of *Balance Like a Pirate*.

It's Me is a powerful reminder that every human being deserves to be seen, heard, and valued for who they are. It is not enough to tolerate or accept someone's individuality. Rather, we must celebrate and appreciate each other for the strengths and talents add to world. *It's Me* is a celebration of those strengths and an appreciation and the differences that make the world a better place. The vignettes are powerful and they are real. And they need to be read by everyone.
-Greg Moffitt, Principal, Equity and Inclusion Champion, Co-Host of #CelebratEd Chat.

EduMatch Publishing

Made in the USA
Monee, IL
23 December 2020